Collectively we're a powerful, positive force.

JEAN REED BAHLE

AMAZING WOMEN
OF WEST MICHIGAN

Text by

Crystal Bowman

with photographs by

Tim Priest

WILLIAM B. EERDMANS PUBLISHING COMPANY

GRAND RAPIDS, MICHIGAN / CAMBRIDGE, U.K.

Published 2006 by
Wm. B. Eerdmans Publishing Co.
2140 Oak Industrial Drive N.E., Grand Rapids, Michigan 49505 /
P.O. Box 163, Cambridge CB3 9PU U.K.

Printed in the United States of America

11 10 09 08 07 06   7 6 5 4 3 2 1

ISBN-10: 0-8028-4022-1 / ISBN-13: 978-0-8028-4022-6

www.eerdmans.com

CONTENTS

v

vi

A NOTE FROM THE AUTHOR

The women featured in this book are truly amazing, and writing their stories was an amazing experience. The women come from all walks of life and differ in age, race, religion, and occupation. Some of the women were born in this community, while others arrived here as refugees, leaving all they had behind in war-torn countries. The diversity that exists among the women is obvious, but the similarities can only be absorbed through hearing their stories.

As I learned more about each woman and attempted to capture her uniqueness on the printed page, a common thread emerged. As each story unfolded, I saw women of courage and determination. Some of the women have earned careers in areas where women previously did not hold jobs, while other women have challenged prejudices and broken through barriers constructed by previous generations. Some of the women have survived life-threatening diseases, while others have refused to be limited by physical circumstances.

Another common element is that of compassion. As each woman follows her heart and pursues her passion, she desires to have a positive influence on those around her and help others live better lives. Whether it is through mentoring, one-on-one counseling, or simply setting a good example, each woman hopes to make a difference in her community by caring about others and changing lives.

The women were willing to share their stories not for personal recognition but rather in hopes of inspiring and encouraging other women in our community. I trust as you read their stories you will appreciate what they, and many others like them, are doing to make West Michigan a great place to live.

CRYSTAL BOWMAN

A NOTE FROM THE PHOTOGRAPHER

When I started this project, I knew I was going to meet some interesting women, but I had no idea how inspiring and phenomenal each of them would actually be. After speaking with each woman individually, to get a feel for the kind of photos I wanted to take, I couldn't wait to get on location and photograph

Photo by Scott Pardon

them. Afterward, it was a very rewarding experience to see the images and the women's personalities come to life. All of these women — with their struggles, accomplishments, and stories — have touched my life in a way that I will remember forever.

TIM PRIEST

AMAZING
WOMEN
OF WEST MICHIGAN

GAIANE AKOPIAN

Gaiane Akopian was only ten years old — a little Russian girl who enjoyed ice skating. But she was noticed by some scouts who were on the lookout for promising ballerinas, and they chose Gaiane to join their professional ballet company. From that day on, the daughter of a Russian mother and an Armenian father was raised to be a ballerina.

After graduating from Yerevan Choreographic College and the Vaganova Ballet Academy in St. Petersburg, Russia, she became the lead dancer in the National Theater Opera and Ballet of Armenia. In 1993 Gaiane was invited to dance at Theater Gera-Altenburg in Germany, where she became known as one of Germany's best dancers. In 1997 her performances in *Romeo and Juliet, Carmen, Swan Lake, Giselle,* and *Cinderella* earned her the title "Dancer of the Year."

"I did not choose to be a ballerina," she explains, "but I fell in love with ballet, and I wanted to dance for the rest of my life." But Gaiane knew she would soon face a tough decision: keep dancing, or become a mom. Most ballerinas do not have children (no tutus in the maternity department!). If they do, it usually marks the end of their dancing careers. "I did not want to give up dancing, but I desperately wanted a child. So I decided to do both." After giving birth to her beautiful son, Artem, she was determined to dance again, with the encouragement of her husband, Akop, and her family. She had a dear friend in Germany named Anahit, who was also a ballerina. The two of them would sip gourmet tea for hours and talk about everything. Anahit was involved in many aspects of the ballet and offered to help Gaiane get back on the stage. "My friend is a beautiful dancer and wonderful spirit who was always by my side. She helped me reclaim my career as a ballerina."

When Gaiane performs on stage, her desire is to connect with people and touch their emotions. She wants them to remember the experience they had while watching her dance. "During a theatrical performance, the audience connects on an emotional level. Regardless of religious beliefs or nationality, the people can share tears and joy and happiness. I wish that experience could be brought into everyday life."

In 1999 Gaiane moved to the United States with her son and her husband to experience a life of freedom and opportunities in a great country. She began dancing in New York, and in 2001 she joined the Grand Rapids Ballet Company — Michigan's only professional ballet company. "I feel very much at home in Grand Rapids. I enjoy seeing different cultures and meeting different people. I am more at home here than any other place I've lived."

Gaiane, Akop, and Artem speak several languages in their home so they can remain multilingual. Even their dog, Marshall, understands English, Armenian, and Russian. The only language Marshall hasn't learned from them is German, so that is what they speak when they don't want him to know what they're saying. It's their secret language.

QUOTE:

It is a fantastic thing to be a woman. Celebrate it!

LYN ANDERSON

Lyn Anderson was raised on the family property known as Tun-Dra Kennels and Outfitters. Her father had a reputation for breeding some of the best Siberian huskies in the world. He was also a founding member of the Iditarod and many other canine organizations. But it was his integrity and strong work ethic that Lyn wanted to model.

When Lyn contemplated careers, she realized the family business was where she belonged. She gradually gained enough experience to take on the responsibilities of puppy placement. "This is a lengthy process which involves many hours of communication with potential owners," she explains. "Huskies are loving and loyal, but they are also strong-willed and independent. They are indoor-outdoor dogs, which means they need the companionship of humans, but since they are strong and active, they need to spend time outdoors every day. I try to make sure our clients understand both the positive and the negative traits of the breed before I release one of our puppies to a new owner."

Many families wishing to own a Siberian husky make several trips to the kennel over a period of months before going home with their puppy. And if Lyn decides a husky isn't right for a particular family or individual, she will let them know. "It's the hardest part of my job," she admits. "But because I take time to develop a relationship with my clients, they usually appreciate my honesty. Before I send them away empty-handed, I suggest other breeds that might fit better with their lifestyle. I often hear from these people later on, thanking me for helping them make the right decision."

Not everyone who comes to Tun-Dra is hoping to own a husky. "One time we had a mom come with her seven-year-old son," Lyn recalls. "He was deathly afraid of dogs because he had been bitten as a toddler. His fear of dogs was a problem because he wouldn't go into anyone's home if they owned a dog. The first time I showed him a puppy, he touched it with his finger and quickly pulled it back. After repeated visits, he became more comfortable with both the puppy and its mother. I could sense that the boy's mom wasn't a dog lover either, but she loved her son enough to go through this process to help him overcome his fears. The best part of the story is that they both fell in love with our dogs and eventually left Tun-Dra with a puppy of their own."

Placing puppies in homes and families is a very rewarding endeavor for Lyn because she knows that her dogs will enable others to live happier, healthier lives. "Each time a client leaves the kennel with a puppy, I know their lives will be enriched — it's a great sense of accomplishment." At the same time, she acknowledges having a bigger goal: "My greatest accomplishment in life will be to have each of my children live a life of faith, integrity, and moral character that will reap many blessings."

4

QUOTE:

Success is being who God created you to be, which may not take you far from home.
But the reward is plain and simple: happiness.

JEAN REED BAHLE

When Jean Reed Bahle has a new batch of students in her acting class at Hope College, she begins with "The Zen Paper Cup" exercise. She tells the students to walk across the studio, one by one, to pick up a paper cup — with their eyes closed. She instructs them not to talk, react, or listen to others, but to focus on traveling between the starting point and the place where they are to get the cup. When none of the students succeed in retrieving a cup, Jean explains that the purpose of the exercise is not to get the cup but to be aware of what was happening on the journey. This exercise triggers a discussion of fear, strategies, anticipation, and all the other emotions we experience in everyday life. She then explains to her students that theatre is about representing life, and the more aware they are, the better actors they will be. "After we do this exercise," says Jean, "the students act as if I've let them in on a secret — which I have!"

Though her passion is teaching theatre to aspiring young students, Jean also enjoys acting, directing, and writing plays. Her acting experiences evolved from her love of singing. "I was a shy kid, but I always enjoyed singing in choruses and small ensemble groups in high school and college. When I started getting lead roles in musicals, I discovered my real love was acting." Since those early days of musicals, she has acted in nearly fifty productions with Grand Rapids Civic Theatre, Hope Summer Repertory Theatre, and Actors' Theatre. Actors' Theatre also gave Jean her first directing op-

portunity two decades ago, and she has been directing plays ever since.

Her playwriting emerged alongside performing and directing. In 1985, Actors' Theatre produced her full-length play called *Ceilings,* and soon after, playwriting became a regular activity for Jean. Local college students have enjoyed performing her series of environmental plays for children, which emphasize positive ways to help the environment. In 1994, Jean was commissioned to write a play called *Invisible Journeys,* which explores the lives of four women from Grand Rapids history. She has also written plays for Hope College, and has taught playwriting at both Hope College and Aquinas College.

Jean is quick to confess that acting, directing, and writing can be exhausting for even the most energetic person. "When I'm tired and don't feel well, I'm tempted to call my voice teacher and cancel my lesson. And then I remember that every time I go and begin singing and breathing and laughing and moving, I always feel better."

Though she has been honored with several grants and prestigious awards, she is involved in theatre simply because she loves it. "There is nowhere in the world I'd rather be. It gets you out of yourself. It's such a balm for the soul and a fire to get you going." Jean enjoys connecting with great people, laughing together, and working hard. She calls it "serious fun."

QUOTE:

I'll see it when I believe it!

AMY BERRIDGE

When Amy Berridge dribbles a basketball or bats a softball, her teammates and her opponents are the same gender she is. But when it comes to competing on a wrestling mat, she faces an opponent of the opposite sex. As an athletic girl, Amy enjoyed being on basketball and softball teams, but her interest in wrestling began as she watched her younger brother compete in this predominately male sport. "When I noticed that there were a few girls who wrestled, I decided that if they could do it, so could I!" She started wrestling in the seventh grade and continued to wrestle in high school with the support of her family, friends, and coaches. As a girl, she had to work hard to be the best wrestler she could be. But she is quick to acknowledge that boys have to work hard as well. "It doesn't matter if you're male or female. We all have to work hard and deal with difficult issues."

In order to wrestle in the individual division at the state meet in her junior year, Amy needed to win a qualifying match against a wrestler to whom she had lost three times before. He was also the only person to pin her in her high school career. "I couldn't believe I had to get past him in order to compete at the state meet, but there was nothing I could do except give it my all!" During the first period of their match, Amy was behind, but she caught up and tied the score in the second period. At the end of the third period,

the tie sent them into overtime. When neither of them scored then, they were forced into a second overtime. "It was getting so intense I felt like my heart was going to jump out of my chest!" recalls Amy. "My opponent was on the mat, and I had to keep him down for thirty seconds. It seemed like the time was going to last forever, and I prayed as every second ticked away. I don't know how, but I did it. When the time ended, I couldn't believe what had just happened! I still get nervous every time I watch the match on video, even though I know the outcome."

Amy was the first girl in Michigan to win a match at the MHSAA Individual State Meet, and the second girl in the nation to place in a state high school wrestling competition. Though she excels in sports and has earned many athletic awards, she is a well-rounded student who has been successful in other areas of her life too. Throughout her high school years, she maintained good grades, served on the student council, was elected class president, and played in the band. She also mentored younger students through a peer-assistance program at her school.

Amy plans to continue her education at Kalamazoo Valley Community College. "With a wide-open future, I want to discover my place in life, achieve my goals, and strive to be the best person that I can be."

QUOTE:
It's not the height, it's the heart.

PAULA BOWERS

As a young girl, Paula Bowers played with dolls like most girls her age. But she also did atypical things. She spent hours in her basement firing pottery in her mother's kiln or sitting outdoors painting pictures from the still lifes her mother set up. Another one of her favorite pastimes was creating woven potholders with interesting patterns — and in her young mind, she was already figuring out how to sell them! But it was her trip to South America as a twelve-year-old that inspired her to make a career of designing tapestry.

"As I traveled through Argentina, Brazil, Peru, and Uruguay, I was fascinated by their handcraft and fiber traditions," Paula remembers. "I saw girls my age weaving intricate patterns with their warps attached to trees. The native Incan women were spinning alpaca with drop spindles while watching their herds. I returned home determined to create my own textured pieces." Paula soon began a twenty-eight-foot jute macramé weaving along a spiral staircase in her parents' home that took her nearly a year to complete and earned her enough money for a trip to Mexico. When her father recognized Paula's passion for this style of art, he helped her build two Navajo looms so she could create her own weavings.

During her college years, she completed European studies and also earned a bachelor of fine arts degree in weaving and fabric design at the University of Michigan. Her work soon appeared in exhibitions and art shows, and she began creating tapestries for residential and commercial use. "When my husband and I were living in Nashville, I designed a tapestry for a major corporation. I was honored when the mayor unveiled my work of art to the public — it was a huge boost to my career! Wherever we lived I tried to make new contacts and create new work."

In 1991 she moved to the Grand Rapids area. In the years that followed, she had two daughters and went through a divorce. "Circumstances in my life changed, so I made some adjustments to meet the needs of my family. I couldn't travel to acquire work as I had before, and I needed a steady paycheck." A manager's position with a custom carpet company proved to be a perfect fit, since she already knew the architects and designers she'd be working with to create rug designs for clients. While she enjoys her job by day, in the evening Paula works on her own projects at the dining room table, with her daughters by her side doing their homework. "Juggling family and career is challenging, but I hope in some way I can encourage other single moms to find that balance between work and being at home."

Paula volunteers for several local schools, helping elementary students create art sculptures. "I feel it's important to give something back to my community and try to inspire the next generation," she explains. She also inspires the next generation by welcoming her daughters' friends into her home, which also serves as her studio and art gallery. With so many fun and interesting things to see and do, there's never a dull moment in her house. And anyone who visits her there will soon learn that creating art is not only her work — it's also her life.

QUOTE:

Find a life you love and live it powerfully!

DIANNE CARROLL BURDICK

"I've always been an artist," says Dianne Carroll Burdick. "When I was five years old, I would trace my hands on paper and draw cities or complex worlds inside the hands. Even at Halloween I dressed up as an artist. I wore a black beret and black clothes, and I carried a palette as my prop."

When Dianne was in high school, she had the opportunity to take specialized classes at a junior college. She took a variety of classes, from pottery and anthropology to world religions and creative writing. "This experience opened the door for me to explore new ideas and learn about things I might not have learned otherwise." In her junior year of high school, she traveled with a small group of students and teachers to the Southwest, where they stayed on an Indian reservation for two weeks. "I studied the art culture of the Native Americans. Since I'm part Cherokee Indian, this was very special to me." During high school, Dianne also had the opportunity to study and work for artist-in-residence Joe Kinnebrew through the Grand Rapids Art Museum.

She took her first photography class while attending Western Michigan University, and the camera has been with her ever since. For the past ten years, she has worked as a freelance photographer in the West Michigan community, going on assignments for newspapers, magazines, schools, libraries, and cultural organizations. "Whether it's going to an elementary school to photograph an author's visit or taking photos at the opera, I always try to capture the emotions of that moment. When my photos end up in a newspaper, they need to grab the reader's attention. When a reader emotionally connects with a photograph, he or she is more likely to read the article."

Though her photographs are masterpieces in and of themselves, she can't leave well enough alone. She has experimented with color by hand-coloring her black-and-white photos to produce breathtaking pictures. *Listen to the Landscape,* a collaboration between Grand Rapids poet Linda Nemec Foster and Dianne, combines Linda's poetry with Dianne's hand-colored photographs. "The poetry reflects the art, and the art reflects the poetry," Dianne explains. "It's a book that transcends race, religion, and culture and can be appreciated by people of all ages and all walks of life. I consider it one of my greatest achievements."

Dianne's work has been displayed in numerous art exhibits, galleries, bookstores, and hospitals. She has earned over twenty awards and was the first photographer to receive the Best of Show award at the Grand Rapids Festival of Arts in 1989. She won the same award again in 1996. "The awards I've received over the years have been humbling, but also rewarding. As a woman I have worked hard in the world of photography. I try to bring a level of intuition to every image so that a truth is revealed. My greatest reward is when something in the image resonates with the client."

QUOTE:
Follow your dream. There will always be hurdles and speed bumps — go beyond all that.

PAMELA CARRIER

How did a small-town girl become a big-city police officer? It wasn't easy, Pamela Carrier says. "I grew up sheltered from the 'real' world. I had to learn that not everyone had the same upbringing I did, and that even though others may have been raised differently, it was not necessarily wrong." She also had to convince others that even though she was a female, she was serious about becoming a police officer. With relentless determination she proved that she was competent for the job, which was evidenced as she achieved her goal of a career in law enforcement. She also blazed the trail and opened doors that helped other women attain positions in law enforcement.

During her tenure with the Grand Rapids Police Department, Pamela was the first woman to work in undercover narcotics. She was one of the first females to earn the ranks of sergeant and lieutenant, and in the department's 134-year history, she was the first female to attain the status of captain. She was also the first woman to be a hostage negotiator, and she has been in charge of the unit for over two decades. In addition to her duties as police captain, she is a licensed professional counselor and an adjunct professor at Ferris State University, teaching in the criminal justice program.

As a wife and mother of two daughters, she finds it challenging to balance her responsibilities at home with a job that often robs her of emotion. That challenge became vividly apparent the day when, following a maternity leave, she returned to work to testify at a court hearing. "I came into the building to go to court when a captain grabbed me and said that we had a bank robber who was holding five hostages and that I needed to talk to him," Pamela recalls. "I went down to the dispatch office and began negotiating with him. Within thirty minutes he released all of the hostages, and the officers on the scene took him into custody. As soon as I was finished negotiating with the robber, I had to rush to court and testify. I had not even been back to full-duty; I was just coming in to testify. Talk about jumping back into things!"

Pamela is fully aware that what she sees in her job and what people do to each other is not "normal." "My colleagues and I are challenged with the job of trying to make sense of what *is* normal. We see so many tragic things out there that we need to guard our emotions, but we also need to experience our emotions for our own mental health. We need to remind ourselves that every victim deserves to be treated with compassion and respect. It may be our hundredth call, but it may be the victim's first."

Providing the best service possible for the citizens of Grand Rapids is what Pamela strives for in her career as a police officer. Her most satisfying moments come when others know that she cares about them and tries her best to serve them. "You may not feel like you can make a difference in someone's life, but you don't know if you don't try."

14

QUOTE:

Treat everyone with respect. Your reward may come when you least expect it.

Whenever a detour sign sends Karen DeVries down a road she didn't plan on traveling, it reminds her of her life. "I've always known what I've wanted to do and where I've wanted to go," she says. "But I've learned that the timing cannot always be my own and that there are many surprises along the way." Karen wanted to be a teacher, but while attending Oakland University in Rochester, Michigan, she was urged to pursue another course of study. "I was told I'd probably never get a teaching job, and even if I did, the pay would be modest. Though I really wanted to be a teacher, I followed this advice and graduated with a marketing degree." She secured a position with a Fortune 10 company in the Detroit area, enjoying a comfortable salary and frequent travels. She also met a man named Dale, who became her husband in a romantic ceremony in Hawaii.

Back in Detroit, Karen continued her work — that is, until Dale's career took them to Indianapolis. Rather than return to marketing, she pursued her original plan and earned certification in elementary education. She also came to a time in her life when she wanted to have children — but it didn't happen the way she thought it would. "Month after month and year after year, I struggled through the journey of infertility. Those were difficult years, but I learned a lot about being patient and trusting God to unfold his plan." When she and Dale adopted an infant son, she finally became a mother. Three years later, she gave birth to a baby girl. "The processes are different," she explains, "but the bond of love is exactly the same."

Her life changed once again when Dale's job brought their young family to Grand Rapids. She was hired as a part-time kindergarten teacher and quickly adjusted to her new surroundings. "My life was moving along smoothly! I loved our little family. I loved teaching." But when their son was only six years old, she realized that God had a greater purpose in their adoption experience. "Our little boy needed a kidney transplant, and I was a match." Karen's teaching career was put on hold while she donated one of her kidneys through successful mother-son surgeries.

One year after her son's transplant, her mother died of cancer. Soon afterward, Dale's mother died too. "I knew the role of being the strong, wise woman in the family would eventually be mine. I just didn't expect it to happen in my thirties," Karen remarks. As she tried to help her children understand how to work through their grief over the loss of their grandmothers, she was inspired to write a warm, comforting story about heaven. Getting her picture book published was a long and emotional journey, but in September 2003, *Peekaboo, Pearly Moon* appeared on bookshelves all over the country.

With both of her kids in elementary school, Karen returned once again to teaching, earned a master's degree in early childhood development, and began writing teacher resource materials for educational publishing companies. In her spare time she enjoys reading, riding roller coasters, and curling up with a bold cup of hazelnut coffee.

QUOTE:

When unexpected circumstances slow your life, try to be patient,
accepting each day as a gift that God is unfolding just for you.

Can making pottery be life-changing? Mary Doezema knows it can — from firsthand experience. "Just as a lump of clay can be molded and shaped into a beautiful object, so can a human life. I've worked with women who were recovering from substance abuse, and I saw a transformation in their lives. They came to my sessions broken and beaten, but as they learned to create beautiful things, they began to reclaim their confidence and self-respect. It was truly a powerful thing!"

At the Urban Institute for Contemporary Arts in Grand Rapids, where Mary formerly served as Clay Program Director, people from all walks of life came to her sessions eager to get their hands dirty, be creative, and escape the stress of everyday life. Even those who considered themselves to be creatively challenged were pleased with the masterpieces they produced.

Mary became interested in pottery while teaching art classes to junior high students. She and her students enjoyed working with clay, but they didn't have the necessary equipment and materials to make the things they wanted to make. So she helped her eager artists build their own potter's wheel and mix their own glazes. "Sometimes it worked and sometimes it didn't," she admits. "But the fun was in experimenting, and we always took pride in whatever we created."

A graduate of Calvin College, Mary has continued her studies with top-notch artists and teachers, and has attended countless workshops to keep shaping her skills — as well as her pots. Her pottery has been on display in galleries and at art fairs throughout the state, and her talents have been recognized with prestigious awards. But she says the greatest rewards lie elsewhere. "I love the art community in West Michigan and the many teaching venues I have here. My greatest personal rewards have come through my art and pottery classes, where I've connected with people and provided a non-threatening environment to foster creativity and enrich lives."

For many years, her raku workshops in the local schools gave kids a lesson they couldn't learn from a textbook. Mary taught them how to form pieces of pottery from clay, then glaze and fire their pottery in kilns. "It was an intense hands-on procedure requiring team effort," she explains. But while the students became absorbed in the creative process, she enjoyed watching them lose their social inhibitions. "During one of my workshops, an introverted boy became so enthused about the activity that he spent the entire day as my assistant. The other students were quite impressed — it was a real ego-boost for this young man!"

Mary continues to develop new pieces and to display her work at various shows and art fairs, but teaching will always be a part of her life. "I teach art classes in the schools whenever I'm asked, and I even offer raku workshops to businesses. My style of teaching was inherited from my junior high English teacher. She taught me to try new things, to have fun learning, and to do my best. That's what it's all about — and that's what I try to teach others."

QUOTE:

Work for the good of others and love beauty.

MIMI EMIG

Like most women, Mimi Emig understands the importance of physical exercise. Unlike most women, she gets her exercise on her way to work — and since the weather in Michigan can be almost anything, her transportation varies from season to season. "When the sidewalks are dry, I walk, bike, or rollerblade. But in the winter, I strap on a pair of cross-country skis and ski to work." She travels anywhere from five to twelve miles, depending on where she needs to be on a given day. And once at work, she rarely takes the elevator; she climbs dozens of stairs — sometimes up to thirty flights a day. "I don't have time to exercise, so I incorporate it into my daily routine."

As a wife, mother, and physician, she is challenged by her responsibilities and often feels pulled in different directions. She is one of four infectious disease physicians in Kent County, treating everything from tuberculosis and HIV to meningitis and pneumonia. She is the medical director of an HIV clinic that serves about 650 infected patients. She has published a study on West Nile virus cases in Kent County, and has been recognized with numerous awards for teaching medical residents.

Mimi understands the struggles that families face when a family member is sick, especially when it's a child. When her younger daughter was an infant, she suffered from pneumonia and was hospitalized every three weeks for the first seven months of her life. Caring for her daughter was all Mimi wanted to focus on, yet she still needed to be a mom to her other daughter, work whenever possible, and carry on with everyday life. "No one can understand how hard it is to have a sick child unless they've had one. Even my friends didn't realize the anguish I felt during that time in my life. I have great empathy for parents of sick children because I've been there and know what they're going through."

Despite her rigorous schedule, she makes time for personal pleasure. She enjoys traveling to other countries and learning about new cultures. "Turkey and Thailand are my two favorite places so far," she says. "I love traveling because it opens my eyes to other points of view and offers a slower pace of life." She also enjoys volunteering in her daughters' school library and running an inner-city Girl Scouts troop. "My life is about doing what I can to make a difference in the lives of others — whether it's through my medical profession, my volunteer work, or at home. I want to be remembered for enjoying life, teaching others, and skiing to work!"

20

QUOTE:

Choose what is important to you and focus on those things. If you don't like something — change it!
Pick your battles and let the little things slide.

LINDA NEMEC FOSTER

"West Michigan is the center of the universe — it's where I fell in love!" declares Linda Nemec Foster passionately. "I fell in love with poetry. I fell in love with life. And I met a young man in my freshman humanities class who became my best friend — and later my husband."

Linda came to Grand Rapids in 1968 to study at Aquinas College. She left her home and family in Cleveland, Ohio, and made a new life for herself in the world of academics. "I was the first person in my entire extended family to attend college, and the first to go to graduate school." She has always enjoyed reading poetry — the deep stuff by serious poets: Shakespeare and Keats, Emily Dickinson and Walt Whitman, Allen Ginsberg and Sylvia Plath. The poem "Fern Hill" by Dylan Thomas inspired her to write her own poetry, and she also gleaned wisdom from Lisel Mueller, a Pulitzer Prize–winning poet. "She taught me that the most enduring poetry has two important components: the power of language to communicate, and the power of metaphor to instill mystery. Balance communication and mystery, and you'll be able to create a true poem." For the past thirty years, Linda has been creating "true poems" that touch the lives of people, many of whom she has never met.

She sees similarities between poetry and everyday life. "It's about transformation. Any subject matter has the potential to be crafted into a dynamic poem, just like a person's life has the potential to be nurtured and developed into a deep, powerful legacy." As a poet and a mother of two grown children, Linda has done both of these things. Her poetry has been published in books, journals, and anthologies. It has been translated in Europe, exhibited in art galleries, used as inspiration for music composition, and performed on stage. Above all, Linda says, her children, Brian and Ellen, make her proud to be a mom.

One of her poetry books, *Amber Necklace from Gdansk*, has been praised by the critics and nominated for over ten major book awards. The subject matter of these poems is deep and personal — a reflection of her family's experiences as immigrants from Poland. "From loss and discovery, to tragedy and redemption, I reclaim my ethnic heritage as I search for myself in the mirror of my family's history."

Linda enjoys introducing others to the world of poetry, hoping to inspire a few young minds along the way. She teaches poetry workshops in schools, libraries, art galleries, and museums. In addition, she and her husband, Tony, established the Contemporary Writers Series at Aquinas College, where renowned poets and writers come to discuss their work with students, teachers, and the general public — "a dream come true and a great cultural addition to the West Michigan community!" And in 2003, Linda was chosen to be Grand Rapids' first poet laureate by the Humanities Council at the Grand Rapids Public Library.

Linda says the key to balancing a busy life is to keep the proper priorities in focus: faith, family, poetry — and a good sense of humor!

QUOTE:
Poetry, like life, can be filled with the power of transformation.

22

RENEA MICHELLE GEERS

Renea Geers learned a major life lesson when she was still a teenager. "When I was sixteen," she confesses, "I sort of ran away to Europe for a summer. This was my one rebellion as a teenager, and it opened my eyes to a whole new world and a whole new way of living. As Americans, we're so pampered and take so much for granted. Living a full and happy life is not about how much stuff we have, but about how much love we live with."

Renea has had many opportunities to express that love to those around her. She has raised her twin boys as a single mom since they were two years old. She cared for her radiant, full-of-life mother, whose life was cut short by breast cancer at age forty-nine. And she walked beside her beautiful sister, Ronda — who is one of her biggest inspirations — as Ronda struggled with cystic fibrosis until she underwent a successful lung transplant. "I've always said that life should be felt, not just lived. You never know what tomorrow can bring, so you need to live each and every day with love and gratitude."

A few years back, while participating in a painting class, Renea was asked to paint what she wanted more of in her life. She grabbed a few of her colors, gave it some thought, and began painting a large purple swirl to represent passion. Next came a red free-form heart for love that intertwined with the purple swirl. Then she filled in all the little spaces with gold for joy, and she surrounded everything with blue for peace. "That painting became my mantra," she says. "I

hung it in the garage in front of my car so it was the first thing I saw when I left in the morning and the last thing I saw when I came home after a long day. It was a constant reminder to live each day with passion, love, joy, and peace."

Up until 2001, Renea changed her career direction several times. She worked as a hairstylist, a travel salesperson, a sales representative for a local radio station, and a sales representative for a high-end picture-frame molding company. "You could say I had about a three-year attention span for jobs, always moving up the ladder, but never moving forward and not completely at peace."

All that changed on October 23, 2001, when she opened Café Solace in downtown Grand Rapids. The word "solace" means "comfort," and that's what she wants the café to provide. "I realize that I would not be where I am today without the love and support I've received along the way," she says, "and the café is my way of giving something back. It's a place of solace where people come to unwind, find some comfort, and escape the pressures of everyday life — it's like a big hug when you walk in the door. I enjoy meeting new people every day, and the ones who return become like a family. Moving up is no longer important to me because I am moving forward in a way that suits me."

As Renea reflects on life with its ongoing challenges and struggles, she emphasizes her belief that you get what you give, and that attitude is everything. "A positive attitude can change your whole day — or your whole life, for that matter!"

QUOTE:

It's not how far you fall . . . it's how high you bounce.

SUZANNE GEHA

When she became the first woman to anchor the nightly newscasts at six and eleven in West Michigan, the television station wanted Suzanne Geha to wear the same blazers as her male colleagues so she'd seem like one of the guys. She was a woman working in a man's world, but she was not interested in looking, acting, or sounding like a man. What she *was* interested in was proving by example that women could report the news intelligently, accurately, and fairly. "My dad encouraged his daughters to seek nontraditional professions and find their passions. I am passionate about news, and I care how it is reported. Broadcast journalists should simply report the truth. It doesn't matter if they are a man or a woman."

Suzanne followed in the footsteps of her aunt, Helen Thomas, a print journalist for more than sixty years. She covered every president since Kennedy and helped open the door for young females wanting to break into the world of broadcast journalism. Suzanne admits that early in her career she felt the need to prove herself worthy of her position. "In a job that was traditionally reserved for a man, I wanted to be professional, competent, and credible. I was afraid that if I didn't succeed, it would be a setback for women's advancement in broadcasting." After more than three decades on television, she has certainly proven her worth. She has received numerous awards both nationally and locally for her excellence in broadcasting, including an Emmy from the Detroit Chapter of the National Academy of Television Arts and Sciences.

The road to her success wasn't always easy. It took a while for the viewers to get used to a female face on the local news. One viewer scolded her for taking the job away from a man. Another accused her of wanting to earn money to buy a yacht, while a third viewer called just to tell her to straighten the part in her hair! When she reported the news as a pregnant woman, the advice and criticism increased even more. "People love to share their opinions," she says. "But when my babies were born, I was flooded with booties, quilts, and cards from those same viewers."

On the home front, Suzanne is a proud wife and mother. She and her husband, Richard, have shared more than thirty years of marriage. Together they have raised four God-loving, happy, productive children, and, despite busy schedules, they manage to sneak away every now and then. "There's so much to do in our community! We love to take a drive out to the beach to watch a sunset, or hop on our bikes and go for a picnic lunch." But she openly confesses that it's exhausting to juggle a career and family. "We working women create sleepless days and nights for ourselves, breathless chaos and controlled crisis trying to balance it all. But I believe women can enjoy great marriages, rewarding child-rearing years, and fabulous careers — while having the time of our lives. My advice to moms and wives is to pray often, pick your husband well, make your children a priority, and discover your passion. When you do that, you will find the life you were born to live!"

QUOTE:

Nothing is more vital to a free society than truth. It is the responsibility of all citizens, not just journalists, to pursue the truth wherever it may lead. Our liberty depends on it.

PATRICIA A. HAIST

As a twenty-three-year-old graduate from Western Michigan University, Patti Haist found herself in unfamiliar territory when she accepted a job in a small Kentucky town. With a master's degree in clinical psychology, she was hired to provide emotional therapy for families in which a child had been sexually abused. In addition, she assisted in setting up a rape crisis program. "It wasn't anything I sought out," she admits. "I was just there when the opportunities presented themselves." But through her work at the Kentucky clinic, she developed a passion for working with women and children who have experienced the trauma of sexual violence in their lives.

In 1985 she moved to Grand Rapids to work as a therapist in the Child Sexual Abuse Treatment Program for the YWCA. In 1990 the YWCA became the agency that offered county-wide services to victims of sexual assault. Rape crisis services were successfully added to the other YWCA programs, and Patti became the supervisor of the sexual assault program. In 1997 she took on the role of director and was involved in implementing Michigan's first program to provide forensic and medical examinations to sexual assault victims. Since that time, the Nurse Examiner Program has conducted over 2,500 examinations, and has assisted in establishing similar programs throughout Michigan.

Helping women recover from the emotional and physical pain of sexual abuse is a challenging job, but it is also very rewarding. For several years Patti provided therapy for a courageous woman who suffered horrendous sexual abuse. "Through our therapy sessions, this woman has learned how to have a healthy, productive adulthood. She has resolved her trauma and incorporated it into her life. She has made the statement to me (on more than one occasion) that I literally saved her life. That is so overwhelming to me, but it speaks to the power of connecting and the power of listening, accepting, valuing, and simply *being with* another human being."

By the time she was forty years old, Patti was well established in her career. Since her mother was a professional working woman, she had never considered not working. But she added another dimension to life when she gave birth to her daughter, Hannah. "I always knew I wanted to be a mom and was worried that time was not going to be on my side. I am fortunate to have a husband who is understanding and flexible. Working with people in crisis situations makes my schedule unpredictable. He can manage things at home when I am unable to be there. Hannah has added so much fun and playfulness to my life. She teaches me patience and reminds me of the importance of laughter."

QUOTE:
It is so important for women to surround themselves with strong, wise
female friends who support, challenge, and encourage one another.

Janet Haynes keeps an interesting daily journal. "At the top margin there's a small space where I list five things I'm grateful for. They vary from day to day — from the small daily pleasures like Krispy Kremes and a good hair day, to the profound." On Janet's list of the profound are things like her job, her health, her friends, and most of all, her two daughters. "My girls are the joy of my life! Having two adult children whom I like, love, and respect, and knowing that they feel the same about me, is something I consider my life's greatest achievement."

Janet entered the work force at the tender age of fourteen, bringing trays of food to patients in a hospital in Marquette, Michigan, and later working as a ward clerk deciphering doctors' scribbles. "The hospital was full of human interest, excitement, often a sense of urgency — and I enjoyed helping people," she says. "Becoming a nurse was a logical step for me." But after she spent years in the nursing field, Janet's former husband and a family friend persuaded her to go to law school. "Once I got into the practice of law, I realized that I was using the same skills I used as a nurse. There was plenty of human drama, and I could help fix people's problems."

When Judge Dale Stoppels retired in 1988, Governor Blanchard appointed Janet to fill the vacancy. She immediately had to run in a county-wide election to keep the seat, which she has retained for nearly two decades. As a judge, she is still in the business of helping people and solving problems, but she admits that this position has its challenges. "I see so much human tragedy, and there's no way to make all things better. I've often wished for a magic wand that would eliminate the sorrows I see on a daily basis. But there are times when I really do make a positive difference in somebody's life — and for those times I am grateful. When I get a thank-you note from a former delinquent youth with a copy of his fabulous report card, or when my picture ends up in a baby book because I helped in an adoption process, or when someone stops me in the grocery store to tell me that her mother is doing well with her new guardian — that's the big reward in this job."

Besides wanting to help people, Janet has another passion that she shares with a few good friends — tap dancing. "For the past thirteen years I've taken tap dance with a group of friends. My daughters and granddaughters come to our recitals and cheer wildly as we aging tappers walk on stage. We know we're terrible dancers, but we have the best rooting section in the place."

Janet believes that every minute is precious, that people are generally well-meaning, and that life is an incredible gift. She hopes to be remembered for her investment in people — for touching lives and helping those who needed help. She also wants to be remembered for being the oldest surviving woman on earth who could still tap dance right up to her death!

QUOTE:

Go forward with neither foolish optimism nor fiber-sapping pessimism,
but simply with that hard, neutral, unyielding persistence which is the core of survival.

She didn't talk about it for thirty years because she somehow felt responsible for what had happened. Then one evening, at a Take Back the Night rally with three hundred people in attendance, Karen Henry spoke about her experience with rape. "Dozens of women came to talk to me afterward to share their stories of incest and other forms of sexual violence," she recalls. "It made me realize that women are strengthened by each other's words and that we need to talk openly about issues that affect us."

Karen is the founder of the Women's Political Action Network, and co-founder of the Womyn's Action Network and the Grand Rapids Women's Action Council. "I encourage women to get involved in the political process, and I want to address violence against women to let them know that sexual assault is not their fault." She also writes magazine articles and lectures throughout the community to dispel negative stereotypes of Arabs and of women in general.

Her strong identity with her Arab roots led her to volunteer in Middle East refugee camps in the mid-1980s, teaching English to young Lebanese and Palestinian women. "The women were smart, eager, and warm, but were living in poverty and war. They had no electricity or running water, yet invited me to have dinner with them, which they prepared from scratch. We became very close, and when I left they gave me an 18-karat-gold medallion that said *Allah* on it — the Arabic word for God. I cried for days."

In her mid-forties, Karen had an experience with breast cancer that prompted her to volunteer with the Pediatric Oncology Resource Team, offering emotional support to families who have children with cancer or blood disorders. "There is a moment of expectation before I first meet the child and his or her family. Will they accept my presence? Will I say the right thing? Then it all vanishes with the first contact as I become transported into their world and begin developing a relationship. The children and their parents have shown me how a family can pull together after an unwelcome diagnosis and make plans and decisions that no one should have to face."

Besides her volunteer work, she is Executive Director of Grand Rapids Operation Weed and Seed, an anti-crime initiative funded by the Department of Justice. She works to form collaborative relationships with community-based organizations, schools, local government, law enforcement, and faith-based groups to improve the quality of life in designated neighborhoods.

Karen enjoys the many friendships she has formed in her community, and one of her best friends is a dachshund named Chaplin (as in Charlie Chaplin). "Spending time with Chaplin takes me away from daily stress and allows me to completely enjoy the moment. He goes with me to work and attends family parties. I had a birthday party for him a few years ago, and twenty-five people came!"

QUOTE:

Recognize the humor in most situations and laugh out loud. Get together with women friends and talk about everything. Take dogs on walks and enter their world.

ZYRAFETE HOXHA

For nearly two decades, Zyrafete Hoxha experienced the emotional stress of living in the war-torn country of Kosovo. But in the late 1990s, things took a turn for the worse as police began using violence against innocent civilians. In 1998 the Serbian police attacked the city of Rahovec, where Zyrafete lived in a basement for seven days with her family and fifty other people. She remembers that experience vividly. "We had no food, and the children were crying because they were hungry. We couldn't go out, and we had to be very quiet so the police wouldn't find us. One by one the families escaped from the basement and fled to safer villages. My husband and I left with three of our children and wandered in the mountains for twelve hours until we came to a small village. I had an older son and daughter and two grandchildren but had no idea where they were or if they were safe. We stayed for awhile in the village of Mirusha, but soon that became dangerous, and we moved to Krusha."

In the village of Krusha, Zyrafete was overjoyed to find her daughter and grandchildren alive and safe. But for three months she had no word from her son and feared the worst. Then one day she received a phone call from him, telling her that he was in Germany and doing well. When her family received word that it was finally safe to return to Rahovec, they were eager to go back to their home. But their return was not what they had anticipated. "We were devastated to find our house nearly destroyed. There were bullets all through the house, and our personal belongings had been stolen. There was no life left for us there, so we made plans to go to the United Sates."

In August of 1999, Zyrafete came to the United States with her husband and young children. "We knew it would be a safer life for our family and that our children would have a better education," she says. "I am happy living in West Michigan and greatly appreciate the many people who have helped me and my family to adjust to a new culture. The people here are so nice and polite. They have given us jobs and are helping my kids in school. I want to tell other women to be happy with their families and realize how fortunate they are to be living in freedom. They have many options here for themselves and also their children. They should be thankful that their children can get a good education."

Zyrafete works in the cafeteria at an elementary school and enjoys making hot lunches for the children and teachers. In her spare time, she enjoys reading good literature, having guests in her home, and talking on the phone to her daughter in Kosovo, whom she misses very much.

QUOTE:

Be happy with what you have and enjoy your freedom.

SVETLANA JOVANOVIC

Svetlana Jovanovic was raised in a middle-class family: her mother was an accountant and her father worked at the township office. But in the socialist town of Modrica, Bosnia, everyone was middle class. After graduating from high school, Svetlana attended college in Sarajevo to become a school psychologist, and she married a man named Vjeroslav. Unable to find a job in Sarajevo, Svetlana returned to Modrica without her new husband and was hired to work at the same school she had attended as a child. "I enjoyed working with my former teachers, who helped me to start my teaching journey. But then I became pregnant and moved back to Sarajevo to be with my husband."

After her son, Nikola, was born, Vjeroslav obtained a one-room apartment through his company. Svetlana worked part-time at her friend's boutique, and life was good for her young family. In the early 1990s an economic and political crisis led to war in Croatia, and her good life was threatened. "The press warned us about the war and said that all of Yugoslavia was going to explode, but we didn't believe it, and neither did our friends. In the spring of 1992, Sarajevo was separated from the rest of the world, and we were trapped! We lived in a basement for four months because of the constant bombing and shooting. We had no food, water, or electricity. Vjeroslav was forced to join the army, and I had to care for our four-year-old son alone. I tried to be strong enough not to panic. I tried to find food for Nikola and play with the other children in my apartment building. But mostly I just tried to survive."

In July of 1992, she and Nikola left Sarajevo in a convoy that went to Croatia. For five months they stayed with Svetlana's grandparents on an island in the Adriatic Sea. During that time, her father and grandfather both passed away, and her mother was diagnosed with colon cancer. In addition, she didn't know where her husband was, and she had no money. "But at least," she recalls, "I had some family members to live with."

Svetlana and Vjeroslav were reunited in the fall of 1992 and went to Germany, where they lived for five years as refugees. In 1997 they came to West Michigan through immigration services and made a new home in a community they have grown to love. "I love the friendly people here, and the fall colors are magnificent! I love my home, which I redecorate every week without spending any money. I also enjoy cooking for my family and friends — since there was a time when I had no food to cook."

Svetlana teaches English as a second language to elementary students, and in May of 2005 she earned a master's degree from Aquinas College. "I have lived in three different countries and have studied the same subject in three different languages. Each time it was challenging, but I enjoy learning new things." She has also found it challenging to adjust to living in different cultures while maintaining her own culture. When friends ask her how she's managed to survive so many challenges and changes, she replies, "I try to think positively."

QUOTE:

My mother always said, "Zlatna sredina," which means "Stay in the middle and avoid extremes."

SISTER PATRICE KONWINSKI

Some people spend years trying to find their vocation — but not Patrice Konwinski. "I knew I wanted to become a sister when I was finishing my sophomore year at Aquinas College. I entered the Grand Rapids Dominican Sisters in my junior year of college and took my final vows as a sister in 1963." One of eight children, Sister Patrice was raised to be a faithful Christian. Her parents encouraged her to be conscious of her gifts and abilities so she would always be generous in sharing them. "My parents were the most significant influence in my life," she says. "They enkindled in me an ethical framework upon which my philosophy of life has been molded. The religious community that I joined as a young woman further nurtured and supported me on my spiritual journey and in the work I continue to do."

The fact that she is a woman and a Catholic sister has never seemed to deter her in the workplace. Though her order is an order of "preachers," she has always been dedicated to the area of service and compassion. "I've always had a passion to find ways to serve others in a Christian manner. I desire to serve in such a way that those I serve can recognize that they have my respect. If I serve with compassion, understanding, integrity, and honesty, I will communicate that respect to others."

In the 1970s Sister Patrice worked as a health-care administrator in Albuquerque, New Mexico. While she held that position, she directed the administrative activities of eleven department directors and coordinated the clinical activities of the hospital. Shortly after she returned to West Michigan, the Code of Canon Law was changed, allowing persons other than ordained ministers to assume the position of chancellor. In 1989 she became the first woman in the state of Michigan — and only the third in the country — to be appointed to that position.

One of her responsibilities as Chancellor of the Diocese of Grand Rapids is to be a resource to parishes. Since the diocese is sensitive to the needs of various ethnic groups, they worked with the Vietnamese community to help them establish their own parish church. For several months Sister Patrice met with the leaders of the Vietnamese community to assist them in their efforts. After many meetings and much discernment, she helped them find a creative solution. They purchased a Protestant church that they were able to adapt to Roman Catholic guidelines. "We all felt it was a job well done," she says. "I was thrilled to witness the joy and happiness of the Vietnamese Catholics who continue to gather under this roof."

Sister Patrice is grateful for the spirit of generosity and volunteerism in West Michigan communities. "I have always witnessed a readiness and willingness of its citizens to respond to a need. And that makes me proud to serve in West Michigan."

QUOTE:

Women need to recognize their own potential and share their talents and skills in a gracious manner whenever possible.

TERRI LYNN LAND

Terri Lynn Land has strong opinions about what government should be. "Government should be simple and easy for the customer," she says. "An effective government thinks creatively and is open to exploring alternatives to the standard way of doing business. We need to look for new ways to solve the challenges we face — especially in these tight budgetary times." These beliefs are what motivated Terri to seek a career in public service. In November of 2002 she was elected to serve as Michigan's forty-first Secretary of State.

Terri's involvement in politics began in high school, when she worked on the presidential campaign for Gerald R. Ford. "I loved school, especially history and government," she recalls. "These subjects were even more personal to me because I actually knew our congressman, Jerry Ford. We were so proud of how he rose to the occasion during a difficult time, serving first as Vice President and then President after Nixon's resignation. When Ford ran for re-election in 1976, I signed up to volunteer as a 'Scatterblitzer,' which involved going door-to-door in the Midwest states asking for votes. But what really sold me on the political process was participating in the Republican National Convention in Kansas City that year. I was mesmerized by the passion and energy of the volunteers, activists, and candidates. We worked so hard, and even though Ford lost the election, I loved the whole process and have been involved in politics ever since."

Another influential person in Terri's life was a woman named Thelma Schuette, who was vigilant in her efforts to preserve the history of Byron Center. "Thelma triggered my passion for history. Her fight to obtain the old township hall and turn it into a museum was inspiring to me." When Thelma passed away, Terri, still in her teens, took over for her as president of the Byron Center Historical Society and helped complete the restoration of the building.

At the tender age of twenty-three, she ran against a veteran legislator, State Representative Jelt Sietsema. During the campaign she met a man named Dan, who was the township supervisor and truly her best volunteer. While she lost that election, she came out a winner: the following year Dan became her husband.

For eight years Terri served as Kent County Clerk. After running local elections, she soon realized that to truly make an impact on elections, she would need to seek out the position of Secretary of State. "Candice Miller held the office of Secretary of State at the time, and during the last year of her term in office I began campaigning. I promised that Michigan's election process would be fair, accurate, and administered with integrity. It's important to me that every Michigan resident knows his or her vote will count."

Since her years of campaigning for Jerry Ford, she's accomplished much in the political arena, but family relationships have always remained her top priority. "I've been married to Dan for more than twenty years. I love being involved in the lives of our children and extended family — they are the center of my life."

QUOTE:

Never, never, never give up. Be persistent.
Do not let anyone talk you out of your goals or dreams.

40

You can find Katie Mawby's picture in the Michigan Sports Hall of Fame. She holds three world records in water skiing. She's been the World Championship water skier for at least ten years (maybe longer — she's not sure). She was named Athlete of the Week by ESPN. She was named Woman Athlete of the Year twice. She's been ranked first in water skiing, snow skiing, and speed skating events — and, by the way, she happens to be blind.

When Katie was struck with sudden blindness as a teenager, her parents and five siblings wouldn't let her give up on life. "My brothers and sisters inspired me to focus on what I was able to do rather than what I could no longer do," she explains. "They motivated me to finish high school and stay active in sports. My parents taught me to have a fearless trust in God and enjoy life as it comes." With the support of her family, she not only finished high school; she also earned college degrees in psychology, physical therapy, and theology.

She is the first to admit that many people have contributed to her success as an athlete. "For over ten years, my water-skiing coaches have been devoted to training me and have been my guides in jump competitions. My husband, Dave, has been beside me every step of the way — encouraging me and supporting me in everything I do. And I've learned a lot about attitude from other disabled athletes!"

Leader Dogs for the Blind has also played a key role in her everyday life. "My leader dog makes it possible for me to travel independently across town and across the country. My current dog, Tucker, gets me to the starting dock of every water-ski tournament." But when it comes to public places, her dog doesn't always receive a warm welcome. She and her dog have been thrown out of restaurants and hassled at airports. "The law permits me to have my dog with me at all times, but some people don't understand." Still, she believes that most Michiganders are quite friendly. "I like the people here, and I love living near Lake Michigan with its beautiful dunes."

Obviously, there are daily challenges to being blind. Katie gets bruises from bumping into things, and a minor miscalculation can be serious. She recalls the time that, after water skiing, she went into a friend's house to change her clothes. She thought she was going into the bathroom, but instead she fell down a flight of stairs and broke her ankle. "Most people think that water skiing is too dangerous for me, but it's the everyday things that cause the most mishaps."

Katie chooses to live one day at a time, trusting God to help her discover her own path in life. "Despite the brevity of earthly life, I realize that God created me to be someone or to do something for which no other person will ever be created. I appreciate the experiences that have made me who I am today, and I look forward to where I will be tomorrow. I try to take advantage of every opportunity. Time is one of our most precious gifts. It should not be wasted."

42

QUOTE:

It is God's will that we give the little we can each day so that he may multiply our virtues.
To worry about tomorrow would be destructive to today.

MECKER G. MÖLLER

I love the colors of the fall, the inspiring serenity,
the beauty of the skies just before winter comes.
And then my soul rejoices when I see the tulips smiling
as spring is born once again.
This is a canvas of West Michigan.

Ask Mecker Möller a simple question like "What do you enjoy about Michigan?" and she will give you a beautiful poem — it just rolls off her lips. But rich, poetic language is not all there is to Mecker. She is also a surgeon and a musician, with a childhood story that could fill the pages of a novel.

She was born and raised in the mountainous region of northern Nicaragua. With a Danish father and a Nicaraguan mother, she was exposed to a mixture of cultures and interests at an early age. "I spent countless hours paging through my father's medical magazines, and I learned about the arts from my mother. I started writing poetry when I was eight years old, but after school I spent my time dissecting frogs and grasshoppers." When she learned about a disease called cancer — that it was devastating and incurable — she boldly proclaimed to the world, "I'm going to become a doctor and find a cure for cancer!" That's when her journey to become a surgeon began, but there were a few interruptions along the way.

"My world was torn apart when my parents divorced," she explains. "I went to live with my grandmother, who gave me the love and stability I needed. But then I watched her slowly die from this dreaded disease, and my quest for a cure took on personal meaning."

After her grandmother died, Mecker faced another tragedy. "The civil war broke out in Nicaragua. I watched my friends and relatives risk their lives for scraps of food. Bombs and bullets took away part of my home and almost took our lives. I fled to Venezuela with my grandfather. The only thing we brought with us was courage." As she and her grandfather attempted to rebuild their lives in a safer environment, she was able to attend high school and college. When the war ended in 1991, she returned to Nicaragua to go to medical school. During these years of intense academic study, she managed to squeeze in several other pursuits: poetry, theater, music, sports, and student government. She was recognized with both academic and musical honors, and her poetry was published in magazines and anthologies.

Her medical career took her to San Francisco, California, where she worked at Oakland Children's Hospital and also Samaritan House Free Medical Clinic, where she established a breast-care clinic for immigrant, uninsured women. Today, Mecker lives and works in West Michigan, specializing as a resident physician in general surgery. "Surgery is both an art and a science," she says. "I consider surgery my passion and one of my greatest loves."

QUOTE:
Take the roads not taken. Things may be difficult sometimes, but not impossible.
Be part of making a change in the world for good in any field you choose.

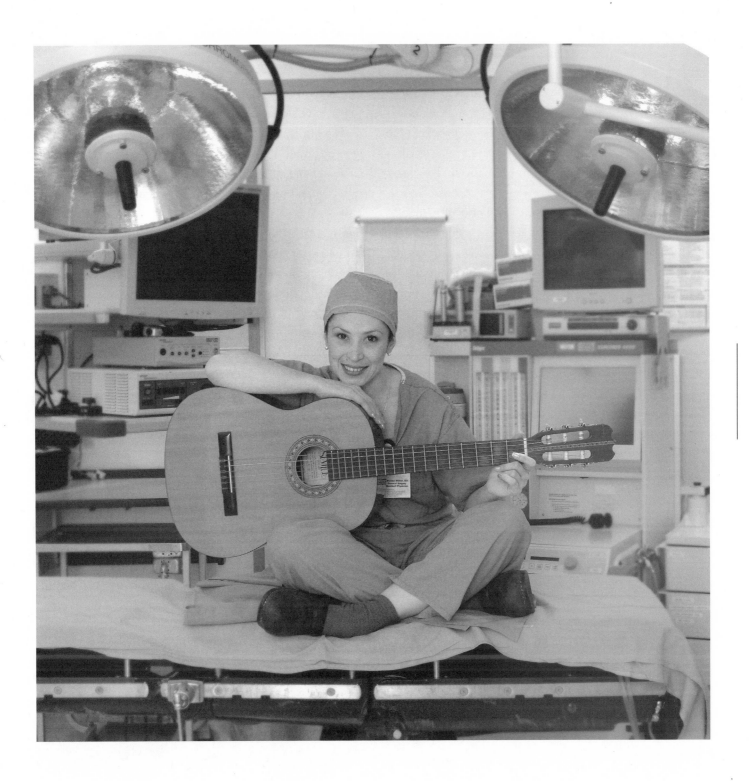

When Ghazala Munir explains her background to American women, her description of her upbringing grabs their attention. "I was raised in a society where males were believed to be superior to females — where the birth of a baby boy was cause for celebration, but the birth of a baby girl was a solemn occasion. My three brothers were always a positive challenge, inspiring me to find my 'place' in a world full of men."

She grew up in the northwest frontier province of Pakistan in the historic city of Peshawar, which borders the beautiful Khyber Pass. As a young girl, she saw women suffer inequality and injustice in every institution. She was only eight years old when she argued with male classmates who believed that because God was a man, he preferred young boys over young girls. "This is what the Muslims in my community believed about God, but it was not the God I envisioned," Ghazala explains. "I argued and fought alone, unable to motivate other girls to stand up against the false assumptions ingrained in their minds by a patriarchal society. My strength and support came from my father, who understood I did not fit the mold. He encouraged me in his quiet and subtle way to seek the ideals of equality and justice. Even though he has passed away, he is still in my heart, encouraging me to go forward and seek my dreams."

In 1967 Ghazala came to the United States and attended high school in Pullman, Washington. She returned to Pakistan to attend college and earned a master's degree in bio-chemistry from the University of Peshawar. In 1973 she came to West Michigan, where her husband accepted a position as a psychiatrist. Her passion continues to be educating young women, especially Muslim women, to recognize their worth as equals in God's creation. "It's up to the younger generation to stand up against the forces of patriarchy and eliminate the injustices done to them in the name of God. In order to ensure that future women live dignified lives, today's women must educate themselves, their daughters, and their granddaughters to reclaim their equality as human beings."

Building bridges between different faith communities in West Michigan has given Ghazala personal satisfaction. "I have been able to reach out to people of faith, from the most liberal to the most conservative." She is one of the founders of Interfaith Dialogue Association and served on its board for several years. She also teaches world religions at Kendall College and is the founder of Gather in Salaam, an educational center for Progressive Islam.

"I realize that I am a little speck in this enormous universe, but hope I have inspired or touched someone's life in some way," Ghazala says. "I trust that my children will be able to love and nurture their own children, and that any achievements in this life will continue to serve humankind in different places and in different ways. I may only be able to make a dent in society, but my work continues until the sun sets one last time."

46

QUOTE:

Deep within our souls, in the inner recesses of our minds, there is a battle being fought every day.
Should we give in to the models society demands us to accept, or should we stand up against them?
I choose not to sell my soul, no matter what the cost.

RONDA PASSON

Determination could be Ronda Passon's middle name. "If someone tells me I can't do something, it makes me want to do it all the more!" she admits. "I'm going to do the things I want to do — like travel, have a career, and jump out of airplanes!" She is known for her positive attitude and strong will. And she is determined to live a full life despite having cystic fibrosis since she was a baby.

After graduating from high school, she wanted to attend college to become a respiratory therapist. Since walking long distances was difficult for her, the obvious solution was to choose a college with a small campus. The strategy worked well, except that one of her classes met on a building's third floor. "When I made a comment about having to hike up three flights of steps, my aunt said, 'Isn't there an elevator you can use?' 'Well, yes, there's an elevator,' I replied, 'but only handicapped people are allowed to use it!' In my mind I was not disabled. I simply made adjustments in my life to compensate for a few minor limitations."

People with cystic fibrosis develop frequent lung infections. Daily therapy is a necessity, but when an infection becomes severe, it's time for an "IV tune-up." Ronda's tune-ups required antibiotic treatments that could be started in the hospital and finished at home. She describes how she handled that. "As soon as I left the hospital, I'd go straight to school or to work and incorporate the IV treatments into my schedule. One time my instructor allowed me to borrow an IV pole from the nursing department and sit in class while hooked up to my IV. These treatments were a part of my life, and I didn't let them get in the way."

Another frustrating thing about having CF is that there are good days and bad days — both of which are impossible to predict. "I hated having to miss important events like my senior-year 'get away' day and my sister's graduation," Ronda says. "Once I had to cancel a trip overseas because the airlines couldn't provide oxygen, and I've also missed a few holidays."

Those bad days, however, are now in the past. In September of 2000, Ronda received a double-lung transplant and is enjoying a life free of fatigue, coughing spells, and frequent trips to the hospital. Within the first year of her surgery, she went on four trips in the States and took a trip to Fiji. She also got married — to a man whose first wife died of cystic fibrosis while waiting for a lung transplant. She and others with CF are sharing their personal stories for an important reason. "We hope that as we share our stories, more people will realize the importance of organ donation and the opportunity they have to give the gift of life to others."

Ronda no longer calculates the walking distance between her car and the grocery store. She no longer drives around parking lots looking for the nearest open spot. "One of my favorite things is driving to Lake Michigan and going for a walk on the boardwalk. I used to stop to cough or catch my breath. Now I only stop to buy an ice cream cone." And as far as climbing two or three flights of stairs goes — no problem! She never took the elevator anyway.

48

QUOTE:

Attitude is 90 percent of the battle. Live. Love. Laugh.

49

Jane Rooks Ross has always been passionate about music. When she was experimenting with the piano as a young girl, that passion expressed itself in an unusual way. "My mother gasped when she saw me coloring on the piano keys!" says Jane. "I had devised this color-coded system to remember the tunes I made up, and coloring the keys was part of my system. Remarkably, my mother understood my intent and showed me how to notate my songs without coloring on the keys."

Jane was raised in a home where music and art were part of everyday life. Her family visited museums and art galleries and listened to music. She attended schools that offered strong art and music programs and was inspired by several high school teachers. "My favorite classes were related to art and music. I loved singing in choirs, studying for my music theory class, and taking art classes with an enthusiastic teacher named Mary Doezema." Jane was one of ten students who spent a week in New York City with their teacher, sleeping on floors in church basements by night and viewing art they had studied in class by day. "It was a formative experience for me. Ms. Doezema was such a masterful teacher that I was inspired to consider teaching as a career."

After earning her degree in music education from Calvin College, Jane entered the career world as a music teacher. She taught general and choral music in the Kalamazoo Christian Schools for fifteen years and was thrilled when the Kalamazoo Symphony Orchestra invited her students to a concert designed for children. "We went to a wonderful concert," she recalls, "but on the way home my students talked about the size of the hall, huge audience, and number of buses, but not about the music! The next year I prepared listening activities for my students based on the concert music. This time my students were excitedly chatting about their favorite music, the sound of the instruments, and the role of the conductor. They had enjoyed a profoundly musical experience."

Jane created listening materials for the Kalamazoo Symphony Orchestra as well as other orchestras across the country. Eventually she applied her teaching background to a new role — as founding Education Director for the Kalamazoo Symphony Orchestra. To encourage a lifelong exploration of orchestra music, she developed many programs, including a traveling, hands-on "Instrument Petting Zoo" and a student composers' competition.

She believes that people of all ages enjoy delving into music, and she has always tried to find ways to increase their enjoyment. "A gentleman once confessed that during concerts he looks at the heads of people in front of him and wonders what they're thinking. I searched for an appropriate book to help him understand the music, but could only find complex music theory and history texts." This prompted her to write *Listener's Guide to the Orchestra*, a booklet now used by orchestras and colleges to explain the basics of orchestra music, describe the instruments of the orchestra, and offer tips for listening. "Empowering people to explore and appreciate music has been a rewarding endeavor for me."

50

QUOTE:
Through music and the arts, we can express and share our deepest emotions,
connect with other cultures and generations, and transcend our limits by experiencing greatness.

VERNIS L. SCHAD

She was trained to work as a secretary. It's what women of her generation were expected to do. But after a year of employment, Vernis Schad left her home in California to attend Calvin College in Grand Rapids, Michigan — a brave move for a young woman in the 1940s. "I chose Calvin because they had a sliding-scale tuition for students coming from a long distance," she explains. "I could also live with a family who provided my room and board." After completing her sophomore year, she chose the typical path of getting married rather than finishing her education. She eventually earned a degree in general studies from Western Michigan University, she notes, "but by then I was so involved in local volunteer work that I continued in that direction rather than find regular employment."

When she enrolled her first child in a public school in Grand Rapids, the principal, Miss Helen Weller, made it clear that all parents were expected to be actively involved. Vernis took that to heart. "I eagerly joined the PTA, volunteered in the lunch room, the library, and helped with many special projects. Before I knew it, I was president of the local PTA, and later, the county-wide organization." During her reign as PTA president, the state passed legislation to reorganize some of the local school districts. She worked to convince voters of surrounding school districts to approve annexation. As a result, the political and geographical area of the core city increased by 50 percent and forever changed the organization of school districts in Kent County.

That experience motivated her to run for election to the Board of Education. During her twelve years as a board member, she faced many challenging issues. "We developed a plan to create a more racially integrated school system, not without some strong objections from both black and white citizens. We replaced neighborhood schools with modern buildings, implemented Title IX to assure gender equality for male and female students, and established some innovative programs that continue to serve special interest students. I am also proud of the fact that during my tenure as board president, the first African American was appointed Superintendent of Grand Rapids Public Schools." Many of the female teachers and administrators appreciated the support given by Vernis and other female board members. "These women often felt ignored, and we tried to make them realize their opinions mattered. We even made it possible for women to sit in the press box during the football games — a privilege previously reserved for men."

As a co-founder of the Women's Resource Center, she has seen many welfare women become independent citizens. She has also been involved with the Greater Grand Rapids Women's History Council, recognizing and celebrating the past accomplishments of many outstanding women. "I want to convince others of the importance of involvement in all kinds of community issues," says Vernis. "I believe that problems in our society can be resolved if citizens express their opinions to elected officials and join organizations working for specific needs."

QUOTE:

*During my life I have experienced more changes than I ever believed possible. To have been a player
in the historical drama of the community has provided pleasant memories to savor for the rest of my life.*

LAURA SCHWENK-BERMAN

Inspired by a performance of *Giselle* danced by Margot Fonteyn and Rudolf Nureyev, Laura Schwenk-Berman decided, at the age of seven, that she had to dance. For fifteen years Laura worked hard as a professional dancer, earning numerous opportunities to perform in ballets throughout the United States and Asia.

While earning a master's degree in theatre from Northwestern University, Laura learned the value of dance as an educational tool for children of all ages. "Every child should have a chance to dance because it can make a difference in their lives," she explains. "Dancing is all the art forms in one because it's visual, it's musical, and it's kinetic. It is athletic, theatrical, and sculptural. Nonverbal communication through movement can be astonishingly beautiful and startlingly honest."

Over the years, Laura has taught ballet and modern dance at a number of colleges, universities, and dance companies. She has worked as a choreographer in Chicago and Grand Rapids, and regularly stages *The Nutcracker* and other works for the Grand Rapids Ballet Company.

Her work at the Grand Rapids Ballet Company, however, has been much more than that of a teacher or choreogra-

pher. With the help of a few determined people, she was able to coordinate efforts to steer the company out of debt, move it to a new building, and catapult it into professional status. Her desire has been to change the perception of dance in the West Michigan area and to make this inspiring art form available to people of all income levels. As she coaches and educates some 275 students, and provides quality educational opportunities with the arts for thousands more, she enjoys watching students grow and develop, as well as giving them opportunities to dance in major companies.

In the non-profit arts world, she knows there is always an endless amount of work that needs to be done. "I've learned not to give up — though it's tempting sometimes," she admits. "I have to constantly remind myself to have the stamina needed to promote change. The discipline of hard work has always paid off for me, not just with success, but with personal satisfaction. My mother taught me to invest in the community that you live in. My work with the ballet company is my investment." To keep from being swallowed up by the demands on her time and to keep her life manageable, she sets priorities. "My husband and children come first, and occasionally I manage to get the laundry done!"

QUOTE:

*The experience of dance nurtures the spirit because it is
the inherent communication between body, intellect, and soul.
It comes closer to the inner language of man than any other form of expression.*

MARY LOU SMITH

There are days when Mary Lou Smith feels as though she's been hit by a truck. When she evaluates the world's situation as well as her personal circumstances, it can easily bring her emotions to the pit. "I've lost family and friends to illness and death," she explains. "And the clueless conduct of business and political leaders is distressing." But when she witnesses talent and insight from young adults, former students, and aspiring performers, she is renewed with hope and reminded that all is not lost.

As an African-American woman raised in the fifties, Mary Lou admits that her choices were limited. "I lived by the strict guidelines applied back then to gender and racial equality, careers, relationships, and financial independence." But with wisdom and guidance from her family and community, she emerged as an educated, talented, contemporary woman. "I admire my parents and ancestors for meeting daunting obstacles with great dignity and good humor. I had teachers open new doors and nudge me through them. And I appreciate the clergy and members of my church for preaching and proving that freedom of thought is a way of life rather than a lofty phrase."

Mary Lou graduated from Aquinas College and studied at Manhattan School of Music and Bank Street College of Education in New York City. As a foreign language major, she received a B.A. in French and loves anything that has to do with language. She taught kindergarten in the Grand Rapids Public Schools for thirty-nine consecutive years. She has performed extensively as a professional accompanist for theater, opera, and ballet companies, and has worked as a coach for classical singers. She has also been a longtime volunteer for the Grand Rapids Symphony and the Grand Rapids Civic Theatre. "Whether I am performing or attending, whether I'm backstage or in a boardroom, I am utterly compelled to set high standards and stay actively involved in the arts."

Being the first black woman to participate in a number of local activities is a source of pride for Mary Lou. But her involvement in everything from dance class in the fifties to Junior League in the seventies was not to advance any particular cause — she simply wanted to be there. "It's important for women to learn what happened before we got here. You're neither the least influential nor the most fabulous female ever to walk the earth. Beware of self-demeaning attitudes, but beware of overblown self-esteem even more," she cautions.

Traveling outside the United States has influenced Mary Lou to see life from another perspective, but so has a serious injury. Living with pain, dependence, and disability on her road to recovery has altered her perspective toward every facet of life — but in her opinion, for the better. "I'd like to make it through life with honesty, humor, optimism, and a sense of style," she says. "And also the ability to see the forest *and* the trees!"

56

QUOTE:

It's always something! (with thanks to Gilda Radner)

57

MICHELLE SMITH-LOWE

Michelle Smith-Lowe believes in the power of imagination. "I believe in imagining a goal, making plans to achieve that goal, and once that goal is achieved, setting the next goal," she explains. One of Michelle's goals was to attend law school and pass the Michigan Bar exam. It was a challenge for the mother of two teenage girls, but it became an even greater challenge when her husband died unexpectedly.

Michelle's husband was the pastor of a local church and a public figure in the African-American community. When he passed away, she not only lost her husband of eighteen years; she also lost her sense of belonging. "It was a painful journey for my daughters and me. We had to find our own identities and realize we were still a family even without a husband and father. I think that's an important lesson for other women as well." Despite the struggles, however, she finished law school, passed the bar exam, and remained active in her church and community.

Michelle worked as a paralegal for several years before becoming a licensed attorney in the trial and labor practice groups of Varnum, Riddering, Schmidt and Howlett. Since 2002 she's been an assistant prosecuting attorney with Kent County, where she handles cases involving child abuse and neglect. "I didn't expect there would be as much abuse and neglect as there is in our community," she admits, "but I am privileged to be a part of a system that helps these children. I have seen everything from deplorable living conditions to shaken babies. I have seen children who were sexually abused by their parents, and I meet mothers who choose men over their children. These children inherit the unresolved issues of their parents and caregivers and deserve a better chance at life. Children deserve to be protected, and they deserve to be in an environment where they are not at risk. Our community is fortunate to have so many service organizations and resources available to assist families with treatment and work toward reunification. We are also blessed to have a number of philanthropic givers that care about making these services available."

Michelle attributes her strength and endurance to her faith in God and also to the values taught to her by her parents and grandparents. "My parents raised me to have a strong relationship with God, to respect and value all people, and to serve mankind in any role necessary. That's the kind of childhood all children deserve, and that's the kind of childhood I've tried to give my daughters."

Over the years, Michelle's family of three has doubled. Besides her daughters, whom she describes as "the best things I have ever had anything to do with," she is proud to include a great son-in-law and precious granddaughter. She is also happily remarried to Bryan, "a wonderful loving, gifted, and talented man" whom she affectionately refers to as her "Boaz."

QUOTE:

Achievement begins by picturing your future and then taking steps to make that picture a reality.

ETHEL FOOTMAN SMOTHERS

"I was never bored," says Ethel Footman Smothers as she re-calls her childhood. "Whether it was flying June bugs or making grass dolls, there was always something to do." Born in rural Georgia in a backwoods section called the Piney-woods, she was the daughter of a sharecropper. When she was seven years old, her family settled in Winter Haven, Florida. "We didn't own a television set, so I entertained my brothers and sisters by telling them stories. I loved making up stories and dreamed of being an author someday."

In 1964 she got married and moved to Michigan, where the change of seasons fascinated this young woman from the South. "Michigan stole my heart from one season to the next," she says. "I love the green summers and the fiery can-opies of color in the fall. On winter mornings frosty patterns of snowflakes are frozen on my window, and then comes spring with new life popping out."

For two decades her focus was on raising her four daugh-ters and being a dedicated wife and mother. "I wanted to raise my girls to love the Lord and do what is right, so they could someday teach their children the same things." But her dream to become an author never faded. She managed to carve out small blocks of time in her busy schedule and began writing stories about her life in the Pineywoods — and she gradually gained enough courage to mail her manu-script to a few major publishers.

When Ethel's first book, *Down in the Piney Woods*, was published in 1992, she became active in the local schools, en-tertaining eager listeners with her captivating stories. "I was living my childhood dream, and it was wonderful!" But two years later, when she discovered a lump in her breast, she began living her worst nightmare. "I felt so ashamed and un-clean. When I knew I would lose my breast to cancer, I didn't want anyone to know. In my culture we didn't talk about things like that. But on the way to the hospital I made a vow to God: 'If you get me through this, I will help other women so they won't have to go through this experience alone.'"

God got her through breast cancer, and she kept her promise. In 1997 she helped establish Sister-to-Sister, a breast-cancer support group devoted to women of color. "I knew of other breast-cancer survivors who saw the need for this type of support group in our community. We needed a program that was sensitive to the cultural and ethnic back-grounds of women of color. Minority women need to know that breast cancer can be talked about — that it is not dirty or shameful. We want to educate them about the disease and offer hope."

Since her recovery from breast cancer, Ethel has written three more children's books and contributed to four women's devotionals. "I have learned to appreciate each new day, to trust God more, and to not take blue skies for granted."

QUOTE:
It's what God knows about you that matters — not what people think.

AMANDA TREVINO

She danced like no one was watching. But somebody *was* watching — a local DJ who noticed Amanda Trevino's exceptional sense of style and rhythm. The DJ approached her and encouraged her to consider becoming a nightclub DJ. "I knew it would be tough to break into this male-dominated career," she says, "but it seemed to be the perfect fit for me."

Amanda began practicing and learning to mix music in a basement, sometimes up to ten hours a day. "There were many times when I was overwhelmed by the whole process," she admits. "I was very tempted to give up, but I refused to quit." Her determination and perseverance paid off when she secured her first gig as an opening DJ at an upscale lounge. Crowds of people began showing up early to watch her perform and listen to her music. Her unique blend of soulful house music along with her playful personality appealed to the listeners, and she quickly developed a loyal following.

"I was thrilled by my local success, but I wanted more," Amanda acknowledges. "I began to learn other styles of music and started performing at a second club. Through endless hours at the computer, I also learned music production and editing, and was hoping to perform in other cities." That hope was realized when, at twenty-three, she was hired to perform at a club in Milwaukee on New Year's Eve. As she waited anxiously for the DJ before her to finish his set, the speakers and monitor blew out. A second monitor was brought in, but after a few minutes that one caught on fire! As Amanda took the stage and put on her headphones, it was clear that she was expected to perform without the necessary equipment. She could hear the music coming into her headphones from the turntables, but she had no idea what she was producing. "It was a frightening experience," she admits, "but the crowd loved the music, so I guess it sounded okay!"

At a time when few females have successfully made it to the top of the DJ world, Amanda stands alone in her market. Today she performs at several clubs, not as the opening DJ but as the headliner, and her performances take her as far as San Francisco and Los Angeles. She plays a wide range of musical formats and has earned great respect from her fans. Her success comes from both her talent and her style. She dares to be a little quirky and doesn't worry about what others think.

62

QUOTE:

Do what you love to do in life and don't let anyone stop you.
Be yourself, be happy with who you are, and live life to the fullest.

VICTORIA UPTON

"I was a pest!" admits Victoria Upton, recalling her childhood years. "I loved being around people and wanted to know everything. I always had a zillion questions!" As a grown woman, she still loves being around people and asking a zillion questions, but she's refined her skills as a pest. She also loves music, art, wearing wild shoes, and trying scary things.

With strong, self-sufficient women in her family, she grew up believing that anything was possible and that everyone should be able to do whatever they wanted to do — as long as it didn't hurt themselves or others. No matter how tough things were in life, she was tougher. But her mother was always standing by, reminding her to be nice. "Being nice was difficult, but I learned it was the smart thing to do!"

In college she changed her mind many times — as well as her major. "First I wanted to be a famous musician, so I majored in music. Then I switched to art, and finally counseling. I was a counselor for fifteen years, which involved drinking coffee and talking to people. I left counseling to work for a local publisher for eight years, and then I started my own business after completing the 'Minding Your Own Business' course offered by GROW [Grand Rapids Opportunities for Women]." Today, as the publisher of *Women's LifeStyle Magazine,* she gets to do what she loves — ask questions, drink coffee, talk to people, and be artistic. And in 2005, GROW honored her with its Business of the Year award.

Her desire to try new things was instilled by her dad, a fun-loving man who wanted his six daughters to be adventurous. "One time I was on the ledge of a mountain, afraid to rappel off," she remembers. "I could hear my dad's voice in my head saying, 'Oh, go ahead — you like scary things!' So of course I did it, over and over again." Victoria tries to learn three new things each year. She recently took up belly dancing, web-site design, and radio programming. Next on the list is rollerblading and learning to sail the sailboat she received for her birthday.

With her optimistic spirit, she knows how to turn challenges into opportunities. One of those challenges is dealing with the amnesia that resulted from a serious illness. She's been faced with relearning many skills and reclaiming part of her past. "I can't remember college boyfriends (maybe that's a good thing!), or being the maid of honor in my best friend's wedding. But I remember most of my childhood, and there are so many new things to learn and discover — that's plenty for me!"

Victoria hopes to make her spot in the universe a nicer place to be. She is doing what she can to make her neighborhood streets safer — like buying a crack house and renovating it to improve the odds of finding more suitable neighbors. She believes in supporting local entrepreneurs by shopping at locally owned markets and stores. There are many things she appreciates about Michigan, but what she likes best is the change of seasons. "Like no other place, we get the four seasons in all of their beauty and intensity." Seems like the perfect place for a beautiful, intense woman!

64

QUOTE:
Well-behaved women rarely make history.
(Laurel Thatcher Ulrich)

POEMA INDIRA WELLER

"Kids teased me about my name, and I planned on changing it when I grew up," confesses Poema Indira Weller. "But after my father died, I came to cherish my name and wouldn't change it for anything. My father was a minister who enjoyed writing poems. He named me Poema, which in Spanish means 'poem,' because he felt I was his best creation."

When she was a teenager, her friends often showed up at her house to seek advice or share their troubles. "My mother wanted to put a sign on my door that said 'free therapy and counseling sessions'!" Poema was only in her twenties when she became the first social services assistant and interpreter for the hospital in Holland, Michigan. She had no formal education or degree to bring to that position, but she performed to her employer's expectations and was able to offer hope to desperate people.

Poema was a social worker for fifteen years, seven of them in a nursing home. She felt that some of the younger residents didn't belong in the home and was determined to find a better placement for them. "I was able to get two brothers in a youth home, another man back home to his family, and another young man transferred to a place where he could attend school," she recalls. "But there was a twenty-seven-year-old quadriplegic who was impossible. The only thing he had control of was his mouth, which he used and abused. I refused to give up on him and finally became his friend." When she suggested to the staff that he needed time alone with his girlfriend, they were horrified. But Poema let the young man visit with his girlfriend in her private office until the staff finally agreed with her. Soon after, the young man married his girlfriend and left the nursing home.

Eventually Poema was dismissed from the nursing home because she didn't have a degree. "I was devastated! But I learned as a child that nothing is impossible if you believe that God will take care of you." After several temporary jobs, she became the purchasing manager of a manufacturing company, earning a comfortable salary and making corporate decisions. She was at the height of her career when budget cuts resulted in the loss of yet another job. Despite this setback, she remained determined. "I decided that same afternoon I was not going to sit home and eat bonbons while watching soaps. I volunteered at an agency called Latin Americans United for Progress — a place where I could help my fellow citizens." Her volunteer position evolved into a part-time job as she turned the agency into a "one-stop-meets-all-needs" type of place where Hispanics can come with their concerns and be treated with dignity.

The greatest difficulty she has faced, she says, also taught her a most precious lesson. "I've faced some tough challenges in life, but my greatest challenge was caring for my dying father. When brain cancer robbed him of his memory, I asked him if he knew who I was. He replied, 'la nena mas linda del mundo,' meaning 'the most beautiful little girl in the world.' Those were his final words. He was the closest thing to an angel on earth. He taught me what unconditional love is all about."

QUOTE:
We know that in all things God works for the good of those who love him.
(Romans 8:28)

66

Being raised in a family with twelve siblings, Rita Williams learned responsibility at an early age. "I was eight years old when my triplet sisters were born. When they were old enough to go for buggy rides, I was allowed to push them around the block. I liked all the attention we got from other people!"

At age fifteen, Rita was certain that becoming a nun was the right path for her, but Mother Victor had other ideas. "She told me I wasn't strong enough to withstand the strain or rigors of life in a convent. It's one of those stories we laugh about at family gatherings." Rita got married at the tender age of nineteen and gave birth to twelve children. "My first and most important job was cast in stone," she says. "Getting twelve children to adulthood safely and hopefully well-balanced was my most challenging and rewarding career. I now have thirty-nine grandchildren and five great-grandchildren who bring me a great amount of satisfaction."

In 1979, when her youngest child was twelve years old, she figured it was time to go back to school. She received an LPN degree and worked at St. Mary's Hospital for five years. She also kept close track of Gill Industries, Inc. — the family-owned manufacturing business that her husband, John Gill, founded with Rita's brother in 1964. "I sat on shop stools, watching, listening, and discussing every aspect of the busi-

ness. After a few years, I was confident that I could make a difference in our male manufacturing world and coaxed John to hire me as general manager. I started by cleaning bathrooms and sweeping corners, and haven't looked back since."

Over the years, Gill Industries has had its share of challenges. Because the company is a product solutions provider for the automotive, furniture, and utility vehicle industries, its success is directly related to the economy. "When customers go bankrupt, or there is a recession or gas crisis, our sales are severely impacted," Rita explains. "In 1998, when General Motors shut down, our company lost several million dollars in sales." But today, as chair and CEO, Rita is pleased to be at the helm of their successful family business. "I'm at a really great time in my life, where it's fun to watch some of the children take over responsibilities for running the business and I'm free to enjoy other activities."

One of Rita's newest passions is owning and operating The Sierra Room — a fine-dining restaurant in downtown Grand Rapids. "John enjoys telling people that I have to work two jobs to support his retirement." Another one of her passions is singing. "I started singing in the choir when I was six years old, and I still enjoy my weekly voice lessons. Singing helps me relax mentally — I think it's what has kept me sane all these years!"

QUOTE:
Always trust your instincts! If you have a gut feeling about something, go with it.
It's great to look ahead and dream. Never stop dreaming, because if you do, a part of you dies.

In Sandy Yeager's senior year of high school, the faculty voted her "Most All-Around Female — Academically and Athletically." At the time she didn't know that these qualities were exactly what she needed for a career as a firefighter. But in 1985, after months of vigorous training, she joined the Grand Rapids Fire Department, where she worked as a firefighter for many years. "This was a great personal achievement for me, since there are so few women in the world of firefighting," says Sandy. Her hard work and determination have also earned her the ranks of Fire Prevention Inspector, Captain of the Fire Prevention Bureau, and Acting Fire Marshal — all of which are unlikely titles for a female.

"People think that being a firefighter is an exciting career of saving lives, but often it's quite the contrary," Sandy explains. "There are those wonderful moments when we can perform CPR and offer life-saving support, but many times when we respond to a call, it's too late, and there is little we can do other than comfort the loved ones and wait for an ambulance to arrive."

When Sandy used to put out house fires with her co-workers, she faced emotional as well as physical exhaustion. "There is nothing more horrible than finding the body of someone who has burned in a fire — especially a child. The only way I could handle it was to focus on the fact that the person was no longer in pain. I'm thankful that I now work in the area of fire prevention, so I can educate others in hopes of preventing these horrifying experiences."

Though Sandy serves the community through her career, she also values volunteer work. For several years she volunteered with FACTS — a mentorship program with the Grand Rapids Public Schools. "I loved developing friendships with the kids and being a part of such an important program. It was a small way to give back to my community and hopefully make a difference in someone's life."

Sandy credits her mother for the strong work ethic she has inherited. "My mother is extremely dedicated. Her love, support, and hard work have provided an example for me to emulate." She also values the friendship of her spiritual mentor, Mildred. "I have been studying with Mildred for ten years, doing a comprehensive study of the Bible. She has helped me to grow immensely in my faith and in my daily walk with the Lord."

Though being Captain of the Fire Prevention Bureau is serious business, Sandy knows how to have fun too. A lover of outdoor activities, she enjoys tubing, gardening, and walking. Her adventures include a white-water raft trip through the Grand Canyon and spelunking in Indiana. She also loves singing and acting, and she performs on stage with Lion Heart Productions. But spending time with her family is always a top priority. "I have a loving husband, Bob, five great kids, and two wonderful daughters-in-law. We are the proud grandparents of an adorable granddaughter. She's the joy of my life!"

70

QUOTE:

Those who hope in the LORD will renew their strength. They will soar on wings like eagles;
they will run and not grow weary, they will walk and not be faint.

(Isaiah 40:31)